Rhyme and Reason Volume 1

A book full of word puzzles

Companion book to poems.limorama.com

GIRIDHAR LANKA

With a foreword by Prof. Leena Chatterjee

To my family

What is 'Rhyme and reason'?

Welcome to a book that does not dictate where to start from and where you end. You can start wherever you like and that does not change what you take away from this small volume.

It has 54 word puzzles based on limericks.

Limericks are 5 anapestic lines following AABBA rhyming scheme. So, line 1, line 2 and line 5 rhyme with each other. Also, line 3 and line 4 rhyme with each other. Line 1, line 2 and line 5 usually have 9 syllables that follow da-da-DUM metre, that's anapest for you. Take the word *unaware* for example. It is pronounced with stress on *-ware.* You have 2 unstressed syllables followed by a stressed syllable. Then, line 3 and line 4 have 6 syllables each. They also follow an anapestic metre.

Let us now tackle the point of rhyming, which is the key point of focus for this book.

One of my close friends, the other day, was surprised when I said "waiting" doesn't rhyme with "biting." In his mind, the ending "ting" was enough. That's how it works in a majority of Indian languages, right? Well, in English, there's another aspect one needs to consider for rhyming. Then you'll understand why "waiting" will rhyme with "baiting" but not with "biting."

That aspect, I now stress, is syllable-stress. For words to rhyme, the syllable in a word that takes primary stress should rhyme, and the following sounds should match (homophonic). Waiting has primary stress on WAIT, so it is WAIT-ing. Biting, on the other hand, is BIT-ing. Now, you can see that WAIT doesn't rhyme with BITE, hence the words do not rhyme though they end with the same suffix, namely "ing."

Let's take another example. "Matter" rhymes with "splatter." It also rhymes with "pat her", which is pronounced as "pat 'er." The second one is a mosaic rhyme or a broken rhyme. There are not many examples of broken rhymes in this volume, so you can safely ignore those for now. That's a set of puzzles for another day and another volume.

Each verse in this book has 3 blanks to be filled. The blank positions are indicated with a number that tells you how many syllables that word has. You will have to figure out the stresses in the syllables based on their position. And to help you, each verse has 3 hints.

Why wait? Dive right in.

Foreword

I have always loved poetry in all its forms and
sizes. From the epics to the haiku, or
the odes, elegies and sonnets, to the ballads,
blank verse or limericks, poetry has
something to offer to every person. For me
poetry has a unique magic that both
triggers the imagination and is food for my
soul. Often poems are layered with
multiple meanings—sometimes obvious, often
hidden—offering new perspectives
with every read. Among the forms, limericks by
Ogden Nash were a personal favourite and
held a special place in my heart. His witty
rhymes and clever humour injected joy into
everyday events and reminded me of the
brilliance in playfulness. When my student
Giridhar Lanka sent me his book Rhyme and
Reason, (Volume1) and requested me to write
a foreword for the book, I was both honoured
and delighted to once again delve into the fun
and enjoyment of limericks.

Limericks have always charmed readers with
their playful rhythm and clever
wordplay. In this book, Giri has brought an
interesting twist to the Limerick, not just

as a source of entertainment, but as a gateway
to learning and discovery. I hope this
will be a hook for the younger generation to
delve more into the magical world of
Poetry.

With 54 limerick-based puzzles, this collection
invites you to delight in the humour,
while exploring the beauty of rhyme, the
subtlety of syllable stress, and the joy of
expanding your vocabulary. Each limerick is
more than just a poetic puzzle; it's an
opportunity to learn. As you solve these
riddles, you will encounter new words,
explore their meanings, and gain a deeper
understanding of how language works.
Whether you're a puzzle enthusiast, a lover of
poetry, or simply curious about the
oddities of English, this collection promises a
unique experience. It offers the joy of
solving, the thrill of learning, and the
satisfaction of seeing how words, sounds, and
meanings come together in delightful ways.

This book encourages you to approach it in
your own way. Start anywhere; this is not
a journey with a set path, but one that rewards
inquisitiveness, patience and a love

for language. Along the way, you will find that
the seemingly light-hearted limerick
holds a surprising depth, combining humour,
rhythm, and reason to both amuse and
Educate.

So, open this book with curiosity and a sense
of adventure. By the time you reach
the last limerick, not only will you have laughed
and puzzled, but also developed a
sharper wit and a richer vocabulary.

Enjoy the challenge!

Leena Chatterjee

Table of contents

26. asonant
27. five-for
28. asocial
29. aspection
30. asphalt jungle
31. aslope
32. assailment
33. Assam
34. assembly language
35. assembly line
36. assembling mark
37. handi
38. at speed
39. among other things
40. amount to anything
41. at someone's command
42. HENRY
43. at someone's bidding
44. at school
45. atsara
46. at present
47. at retail
48. at rest
49. at random
50. at play
51. at someone's suggestion
52. at one's own peril
53. at one's beck and call
54. at no charge

Answers

1. archfoe

He's my enemy number one. _ _,
You will never see both of us _ _ _ _
Any kinship at all.
I can publicly _ _ _ _
Him a jaundiced, resentful archfoe.

This limerick defines the word *archfoe*.

Hint 1: End of line 1 has a mono-syllabic word that rhymes with archfoe. Note that *archfoe* is pronounced with stress on *foe*. So, you should be looking for words rhyming with *foe*. 2 letters!

Hint 2: End of line 2 again has a mono-syllabic word that rhymes with *archfoe* and also the word you filled at the end of line 1. 4 letters!

Hint 3: End of line 4 has a mono-syllabic word that rhymes with all. 4 letters!

As you'd have noticed, limerick has an AABBA rhyming scheme for its 5 lines.

Once you fill all 3 blanks and read the whole verse again, you will see that archfoe is indeed defined in there.

2. Aroras

The Aroras: an Indian class
Of rich merchants. These Hindus _ _ _ _ _ _ _
Most punjabis in _ _ _ _ _ _
They rake in and (ooh, la!)
Preserve all the wealth they _ _ _ _.

This limerick defines the word *Aroras*. Aroras are a
rich class of Punjabi merchants.

Hint 1: End of line 2 has a disyllabic word (with 2
syllables) that rhymes with *class*. Since there are
two syllables in the word you need, the second
syllable should rhyme with *class*. 7 letters!

Hint 2: End of line 3 again has a disyllabic word that
rhymes with *ooh, la*. Ooh, la is pronounced with
stress on Ooh. You're then looking for a word with 2
syllables that sounds like Ooo, la. Simple, isn't it? 6
letters!

Hint 3: End of line 5 has another disyllabic word
and in this case it rhymes with *class* and the word
you zeroed in on in line 2. 4 letters!

There you go! Aroras are very well defined in this
piece.

3. arm's length

When you deal with an entity staying
At an arm's length, it goes without _ _ _ _ _ _
That you're both _ _ _ _ _ _ _ _ _ _ _
And the treatment attendant
On your dealings is equal—no _ _ _ _ _ _ _ _!

This limerick defines the phrase *arm's length.*

Hint 1: End of line 2 has a disyllabic word that
rhymes with *staying.* Since there are two syllables
in the word you need, and the stress in *staying* is
on stay, the first syllable of your answer should also
rhyme with stay, followed by -ing. 6 letters!

Hint 2: End of line 3 again has a tetrasyllabic word
(having 4 syllables) that rhymes *attendant.*
Attendant is pronounced with stress on the middle
syllable, -ten-. You're then looking for a word with 4
syllables with the third syllable rhyming with -ten-.
11 letters!

Hint 3: End of line 5 has another disyllabic word
and in this case it rhymes with *staying* and the word
you zeroed in on in line 2. 8 letters!

That's it! Arm's length is now within your grasp.

4. arrack

In my town near our house, there's a _ _ _ _ _.
Every night they make many a _ _ _ _ _
That is free. But we pay
As we guzzle _ _ _ _
Local booze—toddy, hooch and arrack.

This limerick defines the word *arrack*. Arrack is a cheap liquor that is available in Asian countries.

Hint 1: End of line 1 has a mono-syllabic word that rhymes with *arrack*. Since there are two syllables in arrack, and the stress in is on rack, your answer in line 1 should rhyme with *rack*. 5 letters!

Hint 2: End of line 2 again has a mono-syllable word that rhymes with *arrack* and the word you have found in line 1. 5 letters!

Hint 3: End of line 4 has a disyllabic word and it rhymes with *pay*. As there are 2 syllables in your answer, the second syllable should rhyme with *pay*. 4 letters!

Bingo! You're ready to drink in the results of your efforts.

5. as a child

I'd a mischievous streak as a child.
On occasion, it bordered on _ _ _ _.
Such behaviour _ _ _ _ _ _ _
From a kid, problematic,
Got my parents exceedingly _ _ _ _ _.

This limerick defines the self-explanatory phrase as a child.

Hint 1: End of line 2 has a mono-syllabic word that rhymes with *child*. 4 letters!

Hint 2: End of line 3 again has a trisyllable word that rhymes *problematic*. The word Problematic is pronounced with stress on -mat-, hence the word you are should have its second syllable rhyming with that sound and followed by -ic . 7 letters!

Hint 3: End of line 5 has a monosyllabic word and it rhymes with *child* and the word you filled for line 2. 5 letters!

Child's play! You now have the answers.

6. apopemptic

At the end of our course, we _ _ _ _ _ _ _
All the words Jane had taught us and tried
Our hand at a _ _ _ _ _ _
Valedictory ditty,
Apopemptic. While singing we _ _ _ _ _.

This limerick defines the word *apopemptic*.

Hint 1: End of line 1 has a disyllabic word that
rhymes with *tried* that occurs at the end of line 2. 7
letters!

Hint 2: End of line 3 again has a disyllabic word that
rhymes *ditty*. 6 letters!

Hint 3: End of line 5 has a monosyllabic word and it
rhymes with *tried* and the word you filled for line 1.
5 letters!

Adios! That worked out neatly for a valedictory
verse .

7. appearances to the contrary

Our party was finally _ _ _ _ _
Back to power, though appearances (noted!)
To the contrary _ _ _ _ _ _
That we'd surely implode.
Exit polls: where the drubbed were _ _ _ _ _ _ _ _.

This limerick defines the phrase *appearances to the contrary.*

Hint 1: End of line 1 has a disyllabic word that rhymes with another disyllabic word *noted* that occurs at the end of line 2. 5 letters!

Hint 2: End of line 3 again has a monosyllabic word that rhymes *implode.* The stress in *implode* is on the second syllable and hence the monosyllabic word should rhyme with *-plode.* 6 letters!

Hint 3: End of line 5 has a trisyllabic word and it rhymes with *noted*, and the word you filled for line 1. Given the word's position, the second syllable and third syllable together should rhyme with "noted" and the word you filled in line 1. 8 letters!

Looks simple, doesn't it? Contrary to its appearance, it was quite easy.

8. Apinayé

Gesan folks of north central Brazil
Are Apinayé, who _ _ _ _ _
Now were foreign to me.
They'll continue to _ _
'Cause beyond that my knowledge is _ _ _.

This limerick defines the word *Apinayé*.

Hint 1: End of line 2 has a disyllabic word that
rhymes with *Brazil*. As you know, the stress in
Brazil is on the second syllable. 5 letters!

Hint 2: End of line 4 has a monosyllabic word that
rhymes with *me*. 2 letters!

Hint 3: End of line 5 has a monosyllabic word and it
rhymes with *Brazil* and the word you filled for line 2.
3 letters!

Foreigners no more! You are now familiar with the
Gesan folks from Brazil.

9. hand over

"Yield control!" He's been hov'ring and _ _ _ _ _ _ _
_ over
My desk since this morning, _ _ _ _ _ _ _ _ _ over
And over again!
What a beast! Such a _ _ _ _ !
All the work I did, should I be handing over?

This limerick defines the verb *hand over*.

Hint 1: End of line 1 has a disyllabic word that rhymes with *handing*. 8 letters!

Hint 2: End of line 2 has a trisyllabic word that rhymes with *handing* and the word you filled in line 1 . 9 letters!

Hint 3: End of line 4 has a monosyllabic word and it rhymes with *again*. 4 letters!

Got to hand it to you! You've done a fabulous job!!

10. as a matter of course

Our team leader was pink-slipped today,
But we worked in our BAU _ _ _
As a matter of course.
Was there any _ _ _ _ _ _ _
For forgetting him soon? None, I'd _ _ _.

This limerick defines the phrase *as a matter of course*.

Hint 1: End of line 2 has a monosyllabic word that rhymes with *today*. As you might have rightly guessed, the stress in *today* is on the second syllable. 3 letters!

Hint 2: End of line 4 has a disyllabic word that rhymes with *course*. Since the word has 2 syllables, the second syllable should rhyme with course. 7 letters!

Hint 3: End of line 5 has a monosyllabic word and it rhymes with *today* and the word you filled for line 2. 3 letters!

As a matter of course, you've solved this one easily.

11. athrill

With excitement, athrill, he was _ _ _ _ _ _
At ringside. His boy just defeated,
In boxing, a _ _ _ _ _ _ _
And every bit bulkier
Opponent in bouts very _ _ _ _ _ _.

This limerick defines the word *athrill*.

Hint 1: End of line 1 has a disyllabic word that
rhymes with *defeated*. Since the stress in *defeated*
is on the second syllable, your answer should
rhyme with -feated. 6 letters!

Hint 2: End of line 3 has a trisyllabic word that
rhymes with *bulkier*. Another clue, there is just one
letter to change to get your answer! 7 letters!!

Hint 3: End of line 5 has a disyllabic word and it
rhymes with *defeated* and the word you filled for
line 1. 6 letters!

Thrilling, right? Solving this verse was exciting and
fun.

12. as a matter of fact

In that firm, there was nothing I _ _ _ _ _ _ _ —
Corner office, a package that's _ _ _ _ _ _ _ _
With perks and good growth.
Honest truth: I was _ _ _ _ _
To depart as a matter of fact.

This limerick defines the phrase as a *matter of fact.*

Hint 1: End of line 1 has a monosyllabic word that rhymes with *fact.* 6 letters!

Hint 2: End of line 2 has a monosyllabic word that rhymes *fact* and the word you filled in line 1. 7 letters!

Hint 3: End of line 4 has a monosyllabic word and it rhymes with *growth.* 5 letters!

Solving that was cool, as a matter of fact!

13. ascriptive

In the credits page thanking his _ _ _ _ _ _ _
He wrote an ascriptive note. Courses
He taught all had such
Attributions—nice _ _ _ _ _
That his guiding professor _ _ _ _ _ _ _ _.

This limerick defines the word *ascriptive*.

Hint 1: End of line 1 has a disyllabic word that rhymes with *courses*. Another clue, there is just one letter to change to get your answer! 7 letters!!

Hint 2: End of line 4 has a monosyllabic word that rhymes with *such*. 5 letters!

Hint 3: End of line 5 has a trisyllabic word and it rhymes with *courses* and the word you filled for line 1. 8 letters!

We can now ascribe the success of this answer to you.

14. at someone's discretion

What to tip? You think twenty percent?
Ain't that high for the money I _ _ _ _ _?
At a patron's discretion
Is the hoped for _ _ _ _ _ _ _ _ _ _,
I would say. It's my choice and _ _ _ _ _ _ _.

This limerick defines the phrase *at someone's discretion.*

Hint 1: End of line 2 has a monosyllabic word that rhymes with *percent.* Since the stress in percent is on the second syllable, you should be looking for a word that rhymes with -cent. 5 letters!

Hint 2: End of line 4 has a trisyllabic word that rhymes *discretion.* The stress in discretion is on the second syllable. So, your answer should also follow the same pattern. 10 letters!

Hint 3: End of line 5 has a disyllabic word and it rhymes with *percent* and the word you filled for line 2. 6 letters!

That's it! It is my discretion to state that you have done a great job.

15. at someone's disposal

We have plenty of money at our
Disposal. We gaily _ _ _ _ _ _
What we want when we want.
With much gusto we _ _ _ _ _ _
Our wealth from an ivory _ _ _ _ _.

This limerick defines the phrase *at someone's disposal*.

Hint 1: End of line 2 has a disyllabic word that rhymes with *our*. The word can sometimes be pronounced in 3 syllables too, just like our, which can be stretched to 2 syllables. 6 letters!

Hint 2: End of line 4 has a monosyllabic word that rhymes with *want*. 6 letters!

Hint 3: End of line 5 has a disyllabic word and it rhymes with *our* and the word you filled for line 2. 5 letters!

Great! The answer and the meaning of the verse is at your disposal.

16. at someone's earliest convenience

I nicknamed him Bobby, the burliest.
He'd push me to come at my _ _ _ _ _ _ _ _
Convenience without
Entertaining a _ _ _ _ _
I'd be busy. His "soon" was the _ _ _ _ _ _ _ _ _.

This limerick defines the phrase *at someone's earliest convenience.*

Hint 1: End of line 2 has a trisyllabic word that rhymes with *burliest.* 8 letters!

Hint 2: End of line 4 has a monosyllabic word that rhymes with without. Since the stress in *without* is on the second syllable, you need to look for a word that rhymes with *-out.* 5 letters!

Hint 3: End of line 5 has a trisyllabic word and it rhymes with *burliest* and the word you filled for line 2. 8 letters!

At my earliest convenience, I will declare you a winner in solving this verse.

17. at someone's expense

Though he flew at my parents' expense
He behaved in a way that lacked _ _ _ _ _.
While they covered the fare
He made bad jokes at _ _ _ _ _
Expense and embarrassed them. _ _ _ _ _!

This limerick defines the phrase *at someone's expense*.

Hint 1: End of line 1 has a monosyllabic word that rhymes with *expense*. Since the stress in *expense* is on *-pense*, your answer should rhyme with that. 5 letters!

Hint 2: End of line 4 has a monosyllabic word that rhymes with *fare*. 5 letters!

Hint 3: End of line 5 has a monosyllabic word (again!) and it rhymes with *expense* and the word you filled for line 2. 5 letters!

Good work!

18. at someone's heels

At one time in the polls he was racing
Far ahead of his peers in _ _ _ _ _ _ _ _ _ _
The incumbent. He _ _ _ _ _
They are now at his heels
And quite close. A tough fight he is _ _ _ _ _ _.

This limerick defines the phrase *at someone's heels.*

Hint 1: End of line 2 has a trisyllabic word that rhymes with *racing*. Since the stress in *racing* is on the first syllable, the second and third syllables in your answer should rhyme with *racing*. 10 letters!

Hint 2: End of line 3 has a monosyllabic word that rhymes with *heels*. 5 letters!

Hint 3: End of line 5 has a disyllabic word and it rhymes with *racing* and the word you filled for line 2. 6 letters!

You were at the heels of the right answer and got it eventually!

19. at someone's mercy

Our new boss is a madman, I _ _ _ _ _.
We are all at his mercy in there.
Our fates, he controls.
Rakes us over the _ _ _ _
When he wants. We're in hellish _ _ _ _ _ _ _.

This limerick defines the phrase at someone's mercy.

Hint 1: End of line 1 has a monosyllabic word that rhymes with *there*. 5 letters!

Hint 2: End of line 4 has a monosyllabic word that rhymes with *controls*. Since *controls* has the stress on the second syllable, your answer should rhyme with *-trols*. 4 letters!

Hint 3: End of line 5 has a disyllabic word and it rhymes with *there* and the word you filled for line 1. 7 letters!

Mercifully, you got the answer right in the first try!

20. at any hour

We all love to be guests of the Taj:
Wifey gets her fantastic _ _ _ _ _ _ _,
Kids get goodies (so _ _ _ _ !)
Whenever—at any
Hour served by a great _ _ _ _ _ _ _ _ _.

This limerick defines the phrase at any hour.

Hint 1: End of line 2 has a disyllabic word that rhymes with *Taj*. 7 letters!

Hint 2: End of line 3 has a disyllabic word that rhymes with *any*. 4 letters!

Hint 3: End of line 5 has a trisyllabic word and it rhymes with *Taj* and the word you filled for line 2. 9 letters!

Now I know that I can count on you at any hour to solve these puzzles easily!

21. at a run

At a great speed the Doberman _ _ _
To us, baring its teeth. We _ _ _ _ _
To step back, very frightened
With reflexes _ _ _ _ _ _ _ _ _ _
By that dog at a run (with a plan!).

This limerick defines the phrase *at a run*.

Hint 1: End of line 1 has a disyllabic word that rhymes with *plan*. 3 letters!

Hint 2: End of line 2 has a disyllabic word that rhymes with *plan* and the word you filled in line 1. 5 letters!

Hint 3: End of line 4 has a disyllabic word and it rhymes with *frightened*.10 letters!

That was a nice run you had so far and you've successfully maintained the streak. Good show!

22. as distinct from

A free verse as distinct from a blank
One has got no constraints. You can _ _ _ _ _
One up simply by _ _ _ _ _ _ _.
(Make a speech while you're walking!)
For this verse form, the French you should _ _ _ _
_.

This limerick defines the phrase *as distinct from*.

Hint 1: End of line 2 has a monosyllabic word that rhymes with *blank*. 5 letters!

Hint 2: End of line 3 has a disyllabic word that rhymes with *walking*. 7 letters!

Hint 3: End of line 5 has a monosyllabic word and it rhymes with *blank* and the word you filled for line 2. 5 letters!

Your face is now beaming, as distinct from a blank one that one would encounter if one could not solve this!

23. as good as dead

Life support, that is what he is on.
He's as good as dead, sadly. Far _ _ _ _
And beyond any _ _ _ _,
He's a goner for sure.
To his certain demise he is _ _ _ _ _.

This limerick defines the phrase *as good as dead.*

Hint 1: End of line 2 has a monosyllabic word that rhymes with *on.* 4 letters!

Hint 2: End of line 3 has a monosyllabic word that rhymes with *sure.* 4 letters!

Hint 3: End of line 5 has a monosyllabic word and it rhymes with *on* and the word you filled for line 2. 5 letters!

Thank God! My hopes were as good as dead when we started, but you've revived them with your excellent work.

24. ashcake

A delectably savoury cake
That is readied from cornmeal—I _ _ _ _
It on ashes that smolder.
You'll get no cold _ _ _ _ _ _ _ _
When making this bread for my _ _ _ _.

This limerick defines the word *ashcake*.

Hint 1: End of line 2 has a monosyllabic word that rhymes with *cake*. 4 letters!

Hint 2: End of line 4 has a disyllabic word that rhymes with *smolder*. 8 letters!

Hint 3: End of line 5 has a monosyllabic word and it rhymes with *cake* and the word you filled for line 2. 4 letters!

Let me treat you with an ashcake for your work so far.

25. Asokan column

It's Asokan, that column right there
With some Buddhist inscriptions, quite _ _ _ _ .
Found on Indian _ _ _ _ ,
They depict edicts royal
And showcase the stone carvers' _ _ _ _ _.

This limerick defines the word *Asokan column.*

Hint 1: End of line 2 has a monosyllabic word that rhymes with *there*. 4 letters!

Hint 2: End of line 3 has a monosyllabic word that rhymes with *royal*. Take note that in some cases, this word can be stretched to 2 syllables just like soil. 4 letters!!

Hint 3: End of line 5 has a monosyllabic word and it rhymes with *there* and the word you filled for line 2. 5 letters!

Amazing work!

26. asonant

"Is it voiced?" "No, it's not. Like the 'd',
The third letter in Wednesday, you _ _ _ ."
"Then it's asonant." "Guess
It's the same with the '_'
In aisle." "You're right, I _ _ _ _ _."

This limerick defines the word *asonant*.

Hint 1: End of line 2 has a monosyllabic word that rhymes with '*d*'. 3 letters!

Hint 2: End of line 4 has a monosyllabic word that rhymes with *guess*. 1 letter!

Hint 3: End of line 5 has a disyllabic word and it rhymes with '*d*' and the word you filled for line 2. 5 letters!

I am wordless with wonder!

27. five-for

Took four scalps, and I zealously _ _ _ _ _ for
Another one—lustily _ _ _ _ for
A catch from the batter.
Now the nub of the _ _ _ _ _ _ ?
Got fifth wicket, I managed a five-for.

This limerick defines the cricketing phrase *five-for.*

Hint 1: End of line 1 has a disyllabic word that rhymes with *five*. 5 letters!

Hint 2: End of line 2 has a disyllabic word that rhymes with *five* and the word you filled in line 1. 4 letters!

Hint 3: End of line 4 has a disyllabic word and it rhymes with *batter*. 6 letters!

You have a good shot at being the most successful test taker in these verses!

28. asocial

"What's asocial?" "Unsocial, that's it.
Antisocial will doubtlessly _ _ _
The bill too." "You got _ _ _ _ _ _?"
"I'm done, my dear brothers.
I have stretched my poor brain quite a _ _ _."

This limerick defines the word *asocial*.

Hint 1: End of line 2 has a disyllabic word that
rhymes with *it*. 3 letters!

Hint 2: End of line 3 has a disyllabic word that
rhymes with *brothers*. 6 letters!

Hint 3: End of line 5 has a trisyllabic word and it
rhymes with *it* and the word you filled for line 2. 3
letters!

O, brother! You got that totally right.

29. aspection

Aspection: an old word for viewing.
It is also a way of _ _ _ _ _ _ _ _ _
Old appearance for new
In some plants that go _ _ _ _ _ _ _
Cyclic change—nature's way of _ _ _ _ _ _ _ _.

This limerick defines the word *aspection*.

Hint 1: End of line 2 has a trisyllabic word that rhymes with *viewing*. 9 letters!

Hint 2: End of line 4 has a monosyllabic word that rhymes with *new*. 7 letters!

Hint 3: End of line 5 has a trisyllabic word and it rhymes with *viewing* and the word you filled for line 2. 8 letters!

Upon inspection, I find your definition of aspection going in the right direction.

30. asphalt jungle

All the greenery's gone in the city.
What was earlier verdant and _ _ _ _ _ _
Turned into an asphalt
Type jungle. Alas! _ _ _ _ _
Lies squarely with greed, what a _ _ _ _.

This limerick defines the phrase *asphalt jungle.*

Hint 1: End of line 2 has a disyllabic word that rhymes with *city*. 6 letters!

Hint 2: End of line 4 has a monosyllabic word. The rhyming scheme here is what is called a mosaic rhyme or broken rhyme. In such cases, the stressed syllable rhymes in the words and the remaining syllables are homophones (similar sounding syllables like write and right). *Asphalt* is pronounced with stress on As-. In line 4, you have alas, which is pronounced with stress on -las. So, the stressed syllables are taken care of. So, the end of line 4 should have a homophone for -phalt. 5 letters!

Hint 3: End of line 5 has a disyllabic word and it rhymes with *city* and the word you filled for line 2. 4 letters!

You've not broken the trust I placed in you and solved the broken rhymes very easily!

31. aslope

The ladder, aslope 'gainst the wall
Is so placed to prevent a bad _ _ _ _.
Slanted placement's the _ _ _
To support C.O.G.,
Making sure you won't end up _ _ _ _ _ _ _.

This limerick defines the word aslope.

Hint 1: End of line 2 has a monosyllabic word that rhymes with *wall*. 4 letters!

Hint 2: End of line 3 has a monosyllabic word that rhymes with '*G.*' 3 letters!

Hint 3: End of line 5 has a disyllabic word and it rhymes with *wall* and the word you filled for line 2. 7 letters!

I am leaning on you heavily to solve this one easily!

32. assailment

Our top order collapsed. Such a _ _ _ _ meant
That the bowlers were batting. The _ _ _ _ meant
To relax on the benches
Pulled us out of the _ _ _ _ _ _ _ _.
We survived the attacks and assailment.

This limerick defines the word *assailment* in a
cricketing context.

Hint 1: End of line 1 has a monosyllabic word that
rhymes with the stressed syllable in assailment.
That syllable is *-sail-*. 4 letters!

Hint 2: End of line 2 has a monosyllabic word that
rhymes with *-sail-* and the word you filled in line 1. It
also refers to the last few batsmen that are sent to
add runs to the scorecard. 4 letters!

Hint 3: End of line 4 has a disyllabic word and it
rhymes with *benches*. 8 letters!

You have successfully pulled us out of a difficult
situation and sailed nicely through the versified
assailment!

33. Assam

"List some Indian teas that are _ _ _ _ _
By the names of the places they're grown?"
"They're Darjeeling, Assam,
And Munnar," replied _ _ _ ,
"And to countries far-off they are _ _ _ _ _."

This limerick defines the word *Assam*.

Hint 1: End of line 1 has a monosyllabic word that rhymes with *grown*. 5 letters!

Hint 2: End of line 4 has a monosyllabic word (and it is a proper noun) that rhymes with *Assam*. Note that Assam has stress on the second syllable. 3 letters!

Hint 3: End of line 5 has a monosyllabic word and it rhymes with *grown* and the word you filled for line 1. 5 letters!

I raise a toast to your success!

34. assembly language

An assembly type language's low-level
That assemblers compile. Techies _ _ _ _ _
In writing such lines.
Heavy-duty _ _ _ _ _ _ _ _
And commands—these details have the _ _ _ _ _.

This limerick defines the term *assembly language.*

Hint 1: End of line 2 has a disyllabic word that
rhymes with *level.* 5 letters!

Hint 2: End of line 4 has a disyllabic word that
rhymes with *lines.* 7 letters!

Hint 3: End of line 5 has a disyllabic word and it
rhymes with *level* and the word you filled for line 2.
5 letters!

You've programmed a nice solution for this
problem, kudos!

35. assembly line

The aspiring new author _ _ _ _ _ _
The most basic ingredients not
To be passed over surely.
He churned out a _ _ _ _ _ _
Insipid and assembly line _ _ _ _ .

This limerick defines the term *assembly line*.

Hint 1: End of line 1 has a disyllabic word that rhymes with *not*. 6 letters!

Hint 2: End of line 4 has a disyllabic word that rhymes with *surely*. 6 letters!

Hint 3: End of line 5 has a monosyllabic word and it rhymes with *not* and the word you filled for line 1. 4 letters!

That's it! You've lined up a nice solution for a tough problem.

36. assembling mark

For my furniture bought from Ikea
There are markings to give an _ _ _ _
On assembling the parts.
For such work, I've the _ _ _ _ _.
All those marks are a great _ _ _ _ _ _ _ _!

This limerick defines the term *assembling mark.*

Hint 1: End of line 2 has a trisyllabic word that rhymes with *Ikea*. 4 letters!

Hint 2: End of line 4 has a monosyllabic word that rhymes with *parts*. 6 letters!

Hint 3: End of line 5 has a tetrasyllabic word and it rhymes with *Ikea* and the word you filled for line 2. Take note that the stress in *Ikea* is on the second syllable. 7 letters!

You have made a mark for yourself in these types of versified questions.

37. handi

In Indian cooking, a pot
That is used in the kitchen a _ _ _
Is the handi, a dandy
Utensil that's _ _ _ _ _
To make many foods, cold or _ _ _.

This limerick defines the word *handi*.

Hint 1: End of line 2 has a monosyllabic word that rhymes with *pot*. 3 letters!

Hint 2: End of line 4 has a disyllabic word that rhymes with *dandy*. 5 letters!

Hint 3: End of line 5 has a monosyllabic word and it rhymes with *pot* and the word you filled for line 2. 3 letters!

You have handily solved that problem.

38. at speed

If you're zippy and race at speed
Like lightning, you'll take a big _ _ _ _
In marathon races.
That will soon take you _ _ _ _ _ _,
And in running, my friend, you'll _ _ _ _ _ _ _ _.

This limerick defines the term *at speed.*

Hint 1: End of line 2 has a monosyllabic word that rhymes with *speed.* 4 letters!

Hint 2: End of line 4 has a disyllabic word and it rhymes with *races.* 6 letters!

Hint 3: End of line 5 has a disyllabic word that rhymes with *speed* and the word you filled in line 2. 7 letters!

You've solved that nicely and at good speed.

39. among other things

There were several facts that were not
Clearly mentioned. Small points they _ _ _ _ _ _.
Yet I fathomed the gist—
Simple stuff almost _ _ _ _ _ _
among other things I had _ _ _ _ _ _.

This limerick defines the idiom *among other things*.

Hint 1: End of line 2 has a disyllabic word that rhymes with *not*. 6 letters!

Hint 2: End of line 4 has a monosyllabic word that rhymes with *gist*. 6 letters!

Hint 3: End of line 5 has a monosyllabic word and it rhymes with *not* and the word you filled in line 2. 6 letters!

You've done excellently, exceedingly quick and accurately, among other things.

40. amount to anything

"Do you think he'll turn out to be good?"
"He amounting to anything _ _ _ _ _
Surprise me, that's true.
He's an idiot _ _ _
Folks would willingly trust, _ _ _ _ _ _ _ _ _ _?"

This limerick defines the idiom *amount to anything*.

Hint 1: End of line 2 has a monosyllabic word that rhymes with *good*. 5 letters!

Hint 2: End of line 4 has a monosyllabic word that rhymes with *true*. 3 letters!

Hint 3: End of line 5 has a trisyllabic word and it rhymes with *good* and the word you filled in line 2. 10 letters!

Does this amount to anything, you ask? It does, and that's a lot.

41. at someone's command

Although people at David's command
Were stressed out as they failed to _ _ _ _ _ _ _ _ _
His demands, they were staying
Obedient, _ _ _ _ _ _ _
That he'll change. Are their heads in the _ _ _ _?

This limerick defines the idiom *at someone's command.*

Hint 1: End of line 2 has a monosyllabic word that rhymes with *command*. The stress on command is on the second syllable. So, the second syllable of your answer should rhyme with *-mand*. 9 letters!

Hint 2: End of line 4 has a disyllabic word that rhymes with *staying*. 7 letters!

Hint 3: End of line 5 has a monosyllabic word and it rhymes with *-mand* and the second syllable of the word you filled in line 2. 4 letters!

I am available at your command and will provide more questions for you to answer!

42. HENRY

A "high earner, not rich yet" defines
Who I am. Yes, a HENRY who _ _ _ _ _
For a kingly-type life.
Taxes, bills, and much _ _ _ _ _ _
Hinder growth of my wealth (it _ _ _ _ _ _ _ _ _!).

This limerick defines the acronym *HENRY*.

Hint 1: End of line 2 has a monosyllabic word that rhymes with *defines*. The stress on *defines* is on the second syllable. So, the second syllable of your answer should rhyme with *-fines*. 5 letters!

Hint 2: End of line 4 has a monosyllabic word that rhymes with *life*. 6 letters!

Hint 3: End of line 5 has a disyllabic word and it rhymes with *defines*. So, the second syllable of your answer should rhyme with -fines. 8 letters!

Neat job!

43. at someone's bidding

'Twas a union his father arranged.
Marriage vows, at his bidding _ _ _ _ _ _ _ _ _,
Did not last very long.
As the bond was not _ _ _ _ _
The couple were, shortly, _ _ _ _ _ _ _ _ _.

This limerick defines the idiom *at someone's bidding.*

Hint 1: End of line 2 has a disyllabic word that rhymes with *arranged.* The stress on arranged is on the second syllable. So, the second syllable of your answer should rhyme with *-ranged.* 9 letters!

Hint 2: End of line 4 has a monosyllabic word that rhymes with *long.* 5 letters!

Hint 3: End of line 5 has a disyllabic word and it rhymes with *arranged* and the word you filled in line 2. 9 letters!

I'm glad that you answered this one correctly, at my bidding.

44. at school

My parents though normally _ _ _ _
Aren't so when enforcing a _ _ _ _:
No jobs when I'm studying.
"There's no point in you _ _ _ _ _ _ _ _ _
Your time," they exhort, "while at school."

This limerick defines the idiom *at school.*

Hint 1: End of line 1 has a monosyllabic word that rhymes with *school.* 4 letters!

Hint 2: End of line 2 has a monosyllabic word that rhymes with *school* and the word you filled at the end of line 1. 4 letters!

Hint 3: End of line 4 has a trisyllabic word and it rhymes with *studying.* 9 letters!

That's cool!

45. atsara

It's atsara, achara, achar
Or a Pickle. I reached a _ _ _ _ _ _
For Indian eats,
Forsook all the _ _ _ _ _
And picked this preserve in a _ _ _.

This limerick defines the word *atsara* or *achar*.

Hint 1: End of line 2 has a disyllabic word that rhymes with *achar*. Since the stress in *achar* is on the second syllable, *-char*, the second syllable in your answer should also rhyme with *-char*. 6 letters!

Hint 2: End of line 4 has a monosyllabic word that rhymes with *eats*. 5 letters!

Hint 3: End of line 5 has a monosyllabic word and it rhymes with the second syllable in *achar* and the second syllable of the word you filled in line 2. 3 letters!

You're completely in your senses and not pickled. That has led you to answer this one correctly and swiftly.

46. at present

The weather is great, thought the _ _ _ _ _ _ _—
If I find a game bird, at present,
To devour, what a deal!
In a trice, like a _ _ _ _
To his door came a neighbor's large _ _ _ _ _ _ _ _ _.

This limerick defines the phrase *at present.*

Hint 1: End of line 1 has a disyllabic word that rhymes with *present.* 7 letters!

Hint 2: End of line 4 has a monosyllabic word that rhymes with *deal.* 4 letters!

Hint 3: End of line 5 has a disyllabic word that rhymes *present* and the word you filled in line 1. 8 letters!

At present, you're rocking and that is impressive.

47. at retail

We describe these as retailers' prices
('Cause we're selling at retail). These _ _ _ _ _ _
Are from far-offish lands.
All these wholesale _ _ _ _ _ _
For more discounts are dodgy _ _ _ _ _ _ _.

This limerick defines the phrase *at retail*.

Hint 1: End of line 2 has a disyllabic word that rhymes with *prices*. 6 letters!

Hint 2: End of line 4 has a disyllabic word that rhymes with *lands*. 6 letters!

Hint 3: End of line 5 has a trisyllabic word that rhymes prices and the word you filled in line 2. 7 letters!

Nice job!

48. at rest

Being like my amigo's the _ _ _ _.
He is free of anxieties. Blessed
With calmness, _ _ _ _ _ _ _ _ _ _ _,
And placid humility,
Unlike all the rest, he's at _ _ _ _.

This limerick defines the phrase *at rest.*

Hint 1: End of line 1 has a monosyllabic word that rhymes with *blessed. Blessed* is pronounced as *blest* and your answer should rhyme with that. 4 letters!

Hint 2: End of line 3 has a tetrasyllabic word that rhymes with *humility.* 11 letters!

Hint 3: End of line 5 has a monosyllabic word that rhymes blessed and the word you filled in line 1. 4 letters!

I feel at rest seeing your expertise in solving these puzzles.

49. at random

There's no logic, he chose from his _ _ _ _ _ _
Just a few to be present. At random,
He made the decision
With a single _ _ _ _ _ _ _ _ _—
They should all be arriving in _ _ _ _ _ _.

This limerick defines the phrase at random.

Hint 1: End of line 1 has a disyllabic word that rhymes with *random*. 6 letters!

Hint 2: End of line 4 has a trisyllabic word that rhymes with *decision*. 9 letters!

Hint 3: End of line 5 has a disyllabic word that rhymes with *random* and the word you filled in line 1. 6 letters!

Your approach is logical and does not feel like it is a method at random.

50. at play

I heard sounds of some children at play.
What I found later blew me _ _ _ _.
Their comments were glacial
With overtones _ _ _ _ _ _
At play, in that playground _ _ _ _ _.

This limerick defines the phrase *at play.*

Hint 1: End of line 2 has a disyllabic word that
rhymes with *play.* 4 letters!

Hint 2: End of line 4 has a disyllabic word that
rhymes with *glacial.* Glacial is pronounced as
glay-shul and your answer should rhyme with that.
6 letters!

Hint 3: End of line 5 has a disyllabic word that
rhymes with *play* and the word you filled in line 2. 5
letters!

Solving this is a child's play for you, kudos!

51. at someone's suggestion

"Come and work"! At her suggestion I eyed
A job at her firm and _ _ _ _ _ _ _
After adding some sheen,
Based on tips I could _ _ _ _ _
From the Net, to my profile. I _ _ _ _ _.

This limerick defines the idiom *at someone's suggestion.*

Hint 1: End of line 2 has a disyllabic word that rhymes with eyed. 7 letters!

Hint 2: End of line 4 has a monosyllabic word that rhymes with *sheen.* 5 letters!

Hint 3: End of line 5 has a monosyllabic word that rhymes with *eyed* and the word you filled in line 2. 5 letters!

I'm glad you took up, at my suggestion, these puzzles to solve.

52. at one's own peril

The seeds of misgivings were _ _ _ _
Among friends who were thick. At their own
Peril, besties _ _ _ _ _
To embark on a plan
Full of risks and imperilment _ _ _ _ _.

This limerick defines the idiom *at one's own peril.*

Hint 1: End of line 1 has a monosyllabic word that rhymes with *own*. 4 letters!

Hint 2: End of line 3 has a disyllabic word that rhymes with *plan*. 5 letters!

Hint 3: End of line 5 has a monosyllabic word that rhymes with *own* and the word you filled in line 1. 5 letters!

At my own peril, I would have misgivings about your ability to solve these verses.

53. at one's beck and call

A relationship manager bawled,
"I'm at Dave's beck and call. He's _ _ _ _ _ _ _ _ _ _
_
With the notion that _ _ _ _ _ _ _
From the bank would become one
With the aim to assist when he _ _ _ _ _ _."

This limerick defines the idiom *at one's beck and call.*

Hint 1: End of line 2 has a disyllabic word that rhymes with *bawled*. 10 letters!

Hint 2: End of line 3 has a disyllabic word that rhymes with *-come* one. 7 letters!

Hint 3: End of line 5 has a monosyllabic word that rhymes with *bawled* and the word you filled in line 2. 6 letters!

The answers seem to be coming to you and I'm here, at your beck and call, to provide you with more questions.

54. at no charge

As our family boarded the _ _ _ _ _,
The ticketing gent saw the _ _ _ _ _
Contingent and _ _ _
The manservant get
In for free. He was in at no charge.

This limerick defines the idiom *at no charge.*

Hint 1: End of line 1 has a monosyllabic word that rhymes with *charge.* 5 letters!

Hint 2: End of line 2 has a monosyllabic word that rhymes with *charge* and the word you filled in line 1. 5 letters!

Hint 3: End of line 3 has a monosyllabic word that rhymes with *get.* 3 letters!

Well done, Amigo!

Answers

1. archfoe
   He's my enemy number one. So,
   You will never see both of us show
   Any kinship at all.
   I can publicly call
   Him a jaundiced, resentful archfoe.

2. Aroras
   The Aroras: an Indian class
   Of rich merchants. These Hindus
   surpass
   Most punjabis in moolah
   They rake in and (ooh, la!)
   Preserve all the wealth they amass.

3. arm's length
   When you deal with an entity staying
   At an arm's length, it goes without
   saying
   That you're both independent
   And the treatment attendant
   On your dealings is equal—no straying!

4. arrack
   In my town near our house, there's a
   shack.

Every night they make many a snack
That is free. But we pay
As we guzzle away
Local booze—toddy, hooch and arrack.

5. as a child
I'd a mischievous streak as a child.
On occasion, it bordered on wild.
Such behaviour erratic
From a kid, problematic,
Got my parents exceedingly riled.

6. apopemptic
At the end of our course, we applied
All the words Jane had taught us and
tried
Our hand at a pretty
Valedictory ditty,
Apopemptic. While singing we cried.

7. appearances to the contrary
Our party was finally voted
Back to power, though appearances
(noted!)
To the contrary showed
That we'd surely implode.
Exit polls: where the drubbed were
promoted.

8. Apinayé
    Gesan folks of north central Brazil
    Are Apinayé, who until
    Now were foreign to me.
    They'll continue to be
    'Cause beyond that my knowledge is nil.

9. hand over
    "Yield control!" He's been hov'ring and
    standing over
    My desk since this morning, demanding
    over
    And over again!
    What a beast! Such a pain!
    All the work I did, should I be handing
    over?

10. as a matter of course
    Our team leader was pink-slipped today,
    But we worked in our BAU way
    As a matter of course.
    Was there any remorse
    For forgetting him soon? None, I'd say.

11. athrill
    With excitement, athrill, he was seated
    At ringside. His boy just defeated,
    In boxing, a hulkier
    And every bit bulkier

Opponent in bouts very heated.

12. as a matter of fact
In that firm, there was nothing I lacked—
Corner office, a package that's stacked
With perks and good growth.
Honest truth: I was loath
To depart as a matter of fact.

13. ascriptive
In the credits page thanking his sources
He wrote an ascriptive note. Courses
He taught all had such
Attributions—nice touch
That his guiding professor endorses.

14. at someone's discretion
What to tip? You think twenty percent?
Ain't that high for the money I spent?
At a patron's discretion
Is the hoped for concession,
I would say. It's my choice and intent.

15. at someone's disposal
We have plenty of money at our
Disposal. We gaily devour
What we want when we want.
With much gusto we flaunt
Our wealth from an ivory tower.

16. at someone's earliest convenience
I nicknamed him Bobby, the burliest.
He'd push me to come at my earliest
Convenience without
Entertaining a doubt
I'd be busy. His "soon" was the surliest.

17. at someone's expense
Though he flew at my parents' expense
He behaved in a way that lacked sense.
While they covered the fare
He made bad jokes at their
Expense and embarrassed them.
Dense!

18. at someone's heels
At one time in the polls he was racing
Far ahead of his peers in displacing
The incumbent. He feels
They are now at his heels
And quite close. A tough fight he is
facing.

19. at someone's mercy
Our new boss is a madman, I swear.
We are all at his mercy in there.
Our fates, he controls.
Rakes us over the coals

When he wants. We're in hellish despair.

20. at any hour
    We all love to be guests of the Taj:
    Wifey gets her fantastic massage,
    Kids get goodies (so many!)
    Whenever—at any
    Hour served by a great entourage.

21. at a run
    At a great speed the Doberman ran
    To us, baring its teeth. We began
    To step back, very frightened
    With reflexes heightened
    By that dog at a run (with a plan!).

22. as distinct from
    A free verse as distinct from a blank
    One has got no constraints. You can
    crank
    One up simply by talking.
    (Make a speech while you're walking!)
    For this verse form, the French you
    should thank.

23. as good as dead
    Life support, that is what he is on.
    He's as good as dead, sadly. Far gone
    And beyond any cure,

He's a goner for sure.
To his certain demise he is drawn.

24. ashcake
A delectably savoury cake
That is readied from cornmeal—I bake
It on ashes that smolder.
You'll get no cold shoulder
When making this bread for my sake.

25. Asokan column
It's Asokan, that column right there
With some Buddhist inscriptions, quite
rare.
Found on Indian soil,
They depict edicts royal
And showcase the stone carvers' flair.

26. asonant
"Is it voiced?" "No, it's not. Like the 'd',
The third letter in Wednesday, you see."
"Then it's asonant." "Guess
It's the same with the 's'
In aisle." "You're right, I agree."

27. five-for
Took four scalps, and I zealously strive
for
Another one—lustily dive for

A catch from the batter.
Now the nub of the matter?
Got fifth wicket, I managed a five-for.

28. asocial
    "What's asocial?" "Unsocial, that's it.
    Antisocial will doubtlessly fit
    The bill too." "You got others?"
    "I'm done, my dear brothers.
    I have stretched my poor brain quite a
    bit."

29. aspection
    Aspection: an old word for viewing.
    It is also a way of eschewing
    Old appearance for new
    In some plants that go through
    Cyclic change—nature's way of
    renewing.

30. asphalt jungle
    All the greenery's gone in the city.
    What was earlier verdant and pretty
    Turned into an asphalt
    Type jungle. Alas! Fault
    Lies squarely with greed, what a pity.

31. aslope
    The ladder, aslope 'gainst the wall

Is so placed to prevent a bad fall.
Slanted placement's the key
To support C.O.G.,
Making sure you won't end up asprawl.

32. assailment
Our top order collapsed. Such a fail meant
That the bowlers were batting. The tail meant
To relax on the benches
Pulled us out of the trenches.
We survived the attacks and assailment.

33. Assam
"List some Indian teas that are known
By the names of the places they're grown?"
"They're Darjeeling, Assam,
And Munnar," replied Ram,
"And to countries far-off they are flown."

34. assembly language
An assembly type language's low-level
That assemblers compile. Techies revel
In writing such lines.
Heavy-duty designs
And commands—these details have the devil.

35. assembly line

The aspiring new author forgot
The most basic ingredients not
To be passed over surely.
He churned out a purely
Insipid and assembly line plot.

36. assembling mark

For my furniture bought from Ikea
There are markings to give an idea
On assembling the parts.
For such work, I've the smarts.
All those marks are a great panacea!

37. handi

In Indian cooking, a pot
That is used in the kitchen a lot
Is the handi, a dandy
Utensil that's handy
To make many foods, cold or hot.

38. at speed

If you're zippy and race at speed
Like lightning, you'll take a big lead
In marathon races.
That will soon take you places,
And in running, my friend, you'll
succeed.

39. among other things
There were several facts that were not
Clearly mentioned. Small points they
forgot.
Yet I fathomed the gist—
Simple stuff almost missed
among other things I had caught.

40. amount to anything
"Do you think he'll turn out to be good?"
"He amounting to anything would
Surprise me, that's true.
He's an idiot few
Folks would willingly trust, understood?"

41. at someone's command
Although people at David's command
Were stressed out as they failed to
withstand
His demands, they were staying
Obedient, praying
That he'll change. Are their heads in the
sand?

42. HENRY
A "high earner, not rich yet" defines
Who I am. Yes, a HENRY who pines
For a kingly-type life.

Taxes, bills, and much strife
Hinder growth of my wealth (it
declines!).

43. at someone's bidding
'Twas a union his father arranged.
Marriage vows, at his bidding
exchanged,
Did not last very long.
As the bond was not strong
The couple were, shortly, estranged.

44. at school
My parents though normally cool
Aren't so when enforcing a rule:
No jobs when I'm studying.
"There's no point in you muddying
Your time," they exhort, "while at
school."

45. atsara
It's atsara, achara, achar
Or a Pickle. I reached a bazaar
For Indian eats,
Forsook all the sweets
And picked this preserve in a jar.

46. at present

The weather is great, thought the
peasant—
If I find a game bird, at present,
To devour, what a deal!
In a trice, like a meal
To his door came a neighbor's large
pheasant.

47. at retail
    We describe these as retailers' prices
    ('Cause we're selling at retail). These
    spices
    Are from far-offish lands.
    All these wholesale demands
    For more discounts are dodgy devices.

48. at rest
    Being like my amigo's the best.
    He is free of anxieties. Blessed
    With calmness, tranquility,
    And placid humility,
    Unlike all the rest, he's at rest.

49. at random
    There's no logic, he chose from his
    fandom
    Just a few to be present. At random,
    He made the decision
    With a single provision—

They should all be arriving in tandem.

50. at play
I heard sounds of some children at play.
What I found later blew me away.
Their comments were glacial
With overtones racial
At play, in that playground today

51. at someone's suggestion
"Come and work"! At her suggestion I
eyed
A job at her firm and applied
After adding some sheen,
Based on tips I could glean
From the Net, to my profile. I tried.

52. at one's own peril
The seeds of misgivings were sown
Among friends who were thick. At their
own
Peril, besties began
To embark on a plan
Full of risks and imperilment prone.

53. at one's beck and call
A relationship manager bawled,
"I'm at Dave's beck and call. He's
enthralled

With the notion that someone
From the bank would become one
With the aim to assist when he called."

54. at no charge
    As our family boarded the barge,
    The ticketing gent saw the large
    Contingent and let
    The manservant get
    In for free. He was in at no charge.